Bottom's Blessings

Christiana Glorius

BookLeaf Publishing

India | USA | UK

Presentation by *BookLeaf Publishing*

Web: www.bookleafpub.com

E-mail: info@bookleafpub.com

ISBN: 9789363313675

First edition 2024

To my father, who always encouraged me to publish my poetry. Thanks, Dad.

ACKNOWLEDGEMENT

Without my support system, I'm not sure where I'd be. It is a lucky thing to be able to thank your loved ones while they breathe. I thank my wonderful mother for reminding me that I am a jack-of-all, and am resilient through the roughest storms. Patches the Cat, though illiterate, has provided me with more hours of free cuddle therapy than I could ever afford. My husband, who is in the trenches of life with me daily, and who is my battle-buddy and refuge. My son, who though very small, shows me daily that the world is a beautiful and amazing place if I only get out of my own head. Thank you all.

PREFACE

There comes a time in everyone's life when one gets "stuck." For some, it's more than once, but a seemingly continuous journey through the muck of life that can drag us down - with small reprieves to get our heads above the grime to gasp for air. When this inevitability occurs, as Winston Churchill once stated "If you are going through hell, keep going" reminds us that though painful, the main goal should be to move through it. This is always easier said than done. Getting stuck takes many forms; a layoff, a heartbreak, a falling out, debt, being evicted, or losing a loved one. Sometimes it is just the idea that moving on will be more painful than just enduring the present. When ultimately you find yourself on the other side, and give a glance back to the past - you'll see how as some things were falling apart, they laid the foundation for other things to come together. Like silver linings, sometimes you'll find the sparkle of blessings at the bottom - wherein lies the focus of this arrangement.

If you are struggling with depression, resiliency or mental health, there is help.
Please reach out, you matter.

The National Institute of Mental Health

https://www.nimh.nih.gov/health/find-help

Undertow

Swept away
limbs flailing in the surf
Dragged under wave
after wave
Tumbling in silent chaos
Sand blinding, gagging
Ears rushed with the roar of the sea

Just a second to take a breath
Then swept under again
Pulling, dragging
Farther out
Away

To deeper and darker depths
The endless drop below
Reminds you to keep kicking
Keep fighting

Beneath the waves
Your eyes clear
Lungs aching
To see the rippled sun
Fan out to the quiet world surrounding you

And for a moment
You forget you're drowning

Carbon

3

What do you want?
If money meant nothing
If time stopped ticking

What then?
Is your whole being
so wound up
ground down
that you want nothing else

Staring at the remains
of the bonfire
I once was
I spy a glint

I pull from the ashes
a tiny diamond
What's left
of my dreams

Wiping on my shirt
I tuck it in my pocket
and walk away

Delve

Peering up from below
how long have I been here
more than a moment
more than the song
that plays endlessly in my mind
circling circling

Trying to find solutions to problems long gone
but not solved
Things I cannot change
so I stay and I think

Different endings to finished stories
wishing, thinking
Praying to fix the past
so I circle
and circle

Making inroads
deeper and deeper
down into me
how far it goes
I have yet to find
but it is so very dark down here

I just want to go home

Eupnea

5

Holding a breath for so long
spots dance across open eyes
red blush splashed across puffed cheeks
When released
It takes all strength with it

But the relief
the vanished pain
Of holding on
to something
that wasn't meant for you

And to be left open
to what is

Greater Things

Papers litter
my small scattered space
bills, dues, reminders
stress

Is this all
that life can offer

one
thing
after
another

No.

This was not
what I was made for

I was born to sing
to act, to draw
to paint

Dance under the full moon
barefoot
skirt swirled around my waist

Love another with all my heart
my body and soul

Hum serenades
to my little one
soft and low

yes
I was made
for far greater things

and mustn't lose sight
of little joys
this life brings

Pink Slip

Losing one's job
is not a sin
or a failing

It's not a unique experience
or the end of the story

Just the end of a chapter
and a beginning of a new one

An opportunity
to walk in the sunlight
during the day
letting the breeze dry your tears

To call that friend
you've been meaning to see
Read the book
sitting on your nightstand

Explore the city
you commuted through
yet never really seen

Binge that show

Bake that soufflé
Do what you never had time too

then turn the page

Decay

We weep
by the fallen tree
blown over by the storm

What is must have seen
how many generations
sought shelter in it's strong boughs

Established in it's roots
looking towards endless sky
never thinking about the seasons

How it must have held on
against the wet wind
until it couldn't hold any longer

the long
slow fall
to meet the earth
that nursed it as a seedling

but look
gaze silently
as it begins a new life

Insects fly
Mice frolic
The fox claims it's burrow

A seedling sprouts
in the decay

Comforting Me

In the early hours
of the breaking day
when my mind won't rest

I often imagine
the me of the past
and how she would react

26 year old me
would wrap me in a blanket
and tell me to rest

21 year old me
would stoop sit
and pass me a drink

18 year old me
would encourage me
to work harder

13 year old me
would tell me a joke
to make me laugh

6 year old me

would old me close
and pet my head
as I weep

And all of them
believe in the me
that I am becoming

Steps

They say little steps
can add up
even through sand
or snow and rain
through tar that drags you down
and slowly
so slowly
one after the next
almost forgetting
where you are going
you walk onto arrival

Sincerely

15

Don't need to worry about talking too much
laughing too loud
saying what needs said

Tape's off my mouth
Licking sticky tack off my teeth
No need to edit me

What a feeling to be free
No longer chained
Wrists or brains
Tongues and teeth

The real
Sincerely
Me

Digitasy

Digital dreamland
where nothing is real
not bodies
or thoughts
News or debates

Comparison shopping
ones and zeros
0's and 1's
other people's fairytales
you believe are real
the highlight reel
just bait for clicks

But the dopamine's a hit
so we slide and swipe and click
in a digital fantasy
as reality rots around us

A Different Pace

17

Slow days
not like they used to be
but still good

the cat cleaning her fur
the sun passing by
the baby sleeping in the crib

The Visit

Look back
every once in awhile
not to dwell
just to visit

the person you were
the dreams you chased
the people you spent time with

Bittersweet
Beginnings you didn't know
would lead to more
Lasts you never knew were lasts

But then is gone
and here is then
A visit in time
that passed

Welcome

How blessed
to know
that you exist

heart beating in your chest
thoughts in your head
feet on the Earth

You are here for a reason
that you get to discover yourself
a value, a purpose

How exciting

Checklist

too often
we place blinders
over our own vision

reducing life
to a daily checklist
tasks to execute

I don't remember
when I last
romanced my life

like a watercolor
bleeding into existence

reminding me
not to forget to live

On Shoulders of Giants

God blessed
the shoulders on which I stand

The Mother
who taught me how to love

The Father
who showed me perseverance

The Brother
who was my very first friend

The Sister
who reminded me you're never too old to laugh

The Grandmother
who taught me how to work with my hands

The Teachers
who encouraged my aspirations

The Mentor
who taught me to have a cool head in a crisis

The Professor

who showed me how to grow in knowledge

The Thespian
who encouraged my outspokenness

The Manager
who taught me how to to manage

The Husband
who is my refuge

My Child
who shows me the beauty in everything

And many more
who will remain
a part of me

Waiting Room

There is beauty in the wait
time slowing for a minute
the music of tapping toes
books read, clocks admired
the low song of the radio
echoing from another room
the excitement of anticipation
for your turn

Heard

When there is no sight but tears
and the only thing
that escapes your mouth
is a sob
He knows exactly what you pray for,
you are heard

The Last

25

Stop.
When you know it is ending
When you recognize that
this era is over
Take a breath
and say goodbye
a real goodbye
of smiles, and tears, and laughs
hugs and kisses
Allow yourself a last look
You won't regret it

Little by Little

Slowly the dawn comes
and night sneaks into morning
little by little
light finds its way
back into day

Low Tide

A footing found ground
Just a moment to kick off
surface breaking
above desperate lips
that spit and gasp
at salty humid air

Seared eyes blink
at a cloudless sky
sun shimmering
on red puffed cheeks

Adrift far off from shore
split from the riptide's hold
floating limply at the surface

A deep breath
fills tired lungs
To begin
the long swim
back to shore